-17
CC 0192 8

D1650559

Leabharlanna Atha Cliath
HENRY STREET LIBRARY
Inv/92 : 729   Price IR£6.47
Title: THE SIROCCO ROOM
Class: 821 MAC

THE SIROCCO ROOM

Jamie McKendrick

Oxford   New York

OXFORD UNIVERSITY PRESS

1991

Oxford University Press, Walton Street, Oxford OX2 6DP

Oxford New York Toronto
Delhi Bombay Calcutta Madras Karachi
Petaling Jaya Singapore Hong Kong Tokyo
Nairobi Dar es Salaam Cape Town
Melbourne Auckland

and associated companies in
Berlin Ibadan

Oxford is a trademark of Oxford University Press

© Jamie McKendrick 1991

First published in Oxford Poets
as an Oxford University Press paperback 1991

All rights reserved. No part of this publication may be reproduced,
stored in a retrieval system, or transmitted, in any form or by any means,
electronic, mechanical, photocopying, recording, or otherwise, without
the prior permission of Oxford University Press

This book is sold subject to the condition that it shall not, by way
of trade or otherwise, be lent, re-sold, hired out or otherwise circulated
without the publisher's prior consent in any form of binding or cover
other than that in which it is published and without a similar condition
including this condition being imposed on the subsequent purchaser

British Library Cataloguing in Publication Data
McKendrick, Jamie 1955–
The sirocco room
1. Title
821.914
ISBN 0–19–282820–7

Library of Congress Cataloging in Publication Data
McKendrick, Jamie, 1955–
The sirocco room / Jamie McKendrick.
p. cm—(Oxford poets)
I. Title. II. Series.
821'.914—dc20 PR6063.C544S57 1991 90–42990
ISBN 0–19–282820–7

Typeset by Wyvern Typesetting Ltd.
Printed in Hong Kong

To my parents

ACKNOWLEDGEMENTS

Acknowledgements are due to the editors of the following publications in which many of these poems first appeared: *Edible Gold* (Channel 4); *Guardian, London Magazine, London Review of Books, New Internationalist, New Statesman, Numbers, Oxford Magazine, Oxford Poetry, Poetry Durham, Poetry Now, Poetry Review*, and the *Times Literary Supplement*.

Some of the poems collected here won a major Eric Gregory Award in 1984 and appeared in the anthology: *The Gregory Poems 1983–84* (Salamander Press, 1985).

'Ill Wind' won one of the five prizes in the Guardian/WWF Poetry Competition and was included in *The Orange Dove of Fiji* (Hutchinson, 1989).

CONTENTS

I

A Petrified Zoo 3
Ill Wind 4
Frail Weave 5
Separate Strands 7
Erdmöbel und das Mädchen 8
Living in Sin 9
Live Wire 11
& 12
Confession 13
Fetish 14
Signs 16
Cornbride 19
Earthbound 20
Cargo 21
Rite de Passage 22
Mersey Plumage 23
Landing 25

II LOST CITIES

A Lost City 29
Another Lost City 30
Decadence 31
Double Exposure 32
Margin 33
Nostalgia 34
Memory 35
Enclosure 36
News from Nowhere 37

III

Axle-Tree 41
De-Signifiers 43
Time Piece 44
Nothing Really 46
Odrodek II 47
A Czech Education (1948–) 48

In Front of Them 50
Il capitano 51
Sign Language 52
Darkness in the Mezzogiorno 53
Mermaid 54

I

A PETRIFIED ZOO

The passion of the early fossil-hunters
lit up those expeditions—I was avid
as a sculptor for the clink of the cold chisel,
form freed from its occult swaddling.

Carrara's alps of marble could not match
the limestone quarries near Wenlock Edge
for sheer potential. Dwarfed combers in the wake
of the great earth-movers, we would raid
the burial-chambers of the Silurian Age,

besiege life's early types in their last fastness
and load your Corsair's boot with them: the pennant
of a fern waving, trilobites swimming nowhere
fast in a solid ocean, sectioned and blasted

by the bulk excavators. Once I chanced
on an ammonite like a giant ram's curled horn
so deeply bedded in the rock my chisel
made no more impact than a sparrow's beak.

No one believed my outflung arms. Next day
its resting-place had been sheared and carted off
—my dream-find would be ground to caustic dust
then weighed on the scale of a plasterer's hawk.

3

ILL WIND

To talk of the weather was a morbid sign.
The winds blew wherever they wanted to
raining their freight of dust.
A week before, the sirocco had come
with its tiny pouches of sand, transplanting
one grain at a time the whole Sahara;
silting the windows with a fine tan.
But this was a wind from the north that blew
across frontiers, ignoring the Customs.
If it blew somewhere else the papers were glad.

I brushed a spider from the web it'd spun
between my arm and what seemed to be air —
it fell by a thread then hobbled off,
its fifth or its sixth leg giving it trouble.
'Will they survive it all' you asked 'the insects?'
I remembered the mutation-rates we'd studied
of the fruit fly (short-, long- and cross-winged)
and a luminous dream I'd had of origin:
life spiralling out from the cradled cell
through the basking oceanic forms.

And though the leaves were still I heard the wind
snicking the links with its casual shears.

FRAIL WEAVE

By ions or ozone or iodine,
light unimpaired from the horizon—
how the sea signals itself
by an inkling long before
the hightide crashes on the ear and pines
end in plants splayed and hackled
by the seawind is a mystery
as though a sea inside were answering exactly
with its own miniature lapsing crests
wearing away at an interior shore:
sometimes just inches sometimes whole towns
spirited away in the undertow.

*

Its pebble-chafing, bone-comb undertow.
The old edge of Suffolk lies under the sea;
Dunwich capsized from the Commonwealth
keeps its afterlife of hotels, craftshops,
a harmless wry affair, while down the coast
the squat domain of Sizewell
voids its heat through a pipe into the sea.

*

Sea-anglers dot the foreshore, their rods
like the jittery feelers of crayfish
or the dials of a Geiger counter.
But now the whole heath spreads
violet, salt-kissed, tightly curled
on its bed of peat where the ling and the bell
and the cross-leaved heather cling
in dusky mounds to the earth that holds
on an edge, the dearer for its vanishing.

*

By the sea's edge I coveted the mermaid's purse
(egg-case of the common skate) and the sea-pecked
interior shell of the cuttlefish shaped
like a balsawood pelvis—its ghostly bulk
steered through crizzled veils of ink. The low cliffs
are fraying, leaving packed layers of peat
studded with egg-pale stones exposed
like a wall whose verge is
held by the frailest weave of marram grass.

SEPARATE STRANDS

To diminish patiently like the white cliffs!

Your rucksack straps like mangrove shoots
coded with movement take root anywhere:
hammocked above you on the luggage rack
or attached to you not knowing their luck.

On the boat to Ostend, the Munich train
the intimate thread may fray like saliva
in a backdraught or seawind . . . such a
delicate durable cable of twine
unravels like limbs after love; a ladder
of twisted sheets, your long hair in the night.

ERDMÖBEL UND DAS MÄDCHEN

We export our designs to the other world
and expect little in return.
In East Germany the whole range
of funeral accessories is sold
under the sign—EARTHFURNITURE.
Cleanliness is close to us: our rich
dust-free bodies are stored away
where the moth's jaws will never reach
and rust and rot will not corrupt.

Everywhere you go you take
your glossy furniture catalogue
—some cut-price Swedish firm
with its nearest depot in Heidelberg.
The problem is transportation.
You imagine a convoy of lorries
crossing the Alps in solemn formation
measuring the length of Italy
to darken the road outside your door.

LIVING IN SIN

We were never at home in that house, the home
of the Bishop of Truro's widow:
our personalities were too small, our words
seemed to tail off and to touch
was a day's journey across the flowered divan.
When friends came to stay we put on
a brave face, took meals off the oak table
and walked around as if we owned the place.

Even our books were outnumbered and outflanked
by their leatherbound tomes. I felt evil
as a water-spider in an air-bubble
leafing through the annotated Bible
yet I began to understand his recreations
—mainly Daniel and Revelations.
The seven hills of Babylon meant Rome
and, once there, he went to town on scarlet
and fornication, lulling himself with wrath.
666 would ring a bell at
the Pope's bedside or was it upside-down,
I wondered, implicating the police?

Much of it was illegible, but that spiky hand
reached out of the grave with its NBs
and admonitory rapping commentaries
as the Victorian engravings on the stairs
we wanted to, but never dared, remove
had bodies in chaste nightgowns rising from
a host of cracked-asunder sepulchres
lock-jawed, stiff-jointed and justified.

We were thieves that had stolen into the fold
waiting to be discovered and expelled
by a flaming sword. The widow's letter came
more terrible than flames, more tearful
at what I don't think we had meant to hide
—'our situation'. It was clear she saw
the Unclean coupling in the Inner Sanctum,

brazen and tireless and 'under her roof'.
If only what we'd done had given proof
to her acrobatic fantasy, if only
the empty rooms had echoed with our cries
we might have felt less wronged. At the year's end

we were given notice and her middle-aged son,
squinting at us with unspeakable pleasure,
said he was sorry but they'd decided
to sell. He helped me shift the tea-chests
and his eyes fell on your clothes as though dazed
in a perfumed garden. Two weeks later
a young married couple were the new tenants
filling the house, making themselves at home.

LIVE WIRE

A high-wire slung from your living-room
to mine, the phone is our precarious go-between
though the pigeons that hang about the stairwell
of your estate, puffed-up and choleric
like Hitchcock extras, aiming the ambush
of their dishevelled take-offs at eye-level
might be groomed as our dispatch riders
if they'd learn to carry notes instead of
treating the brickwork to dingy graffiti.
I can see long lines of messenger-pigeons
winging their way on intimate errands
across the ragged skyline of Hackney

—a sight quaintly escapist like the mural
your window looks onto, with its lavish
trompe l'œil forest of palm trees and banyans
in colours bright as parrots, moving in
on the courtyard's real impoverished rowans
as though that way to coat a starker need
for more than painted fruit. My need for you,
if now that's what I'm calling it,
is still as clear as that first morning
you left with a promise I guessed would have
me wound by my nerves like a creeper round
the still receiver, willing it to ring.

&

A born rebel, at ease in your outrage
you refuse the armchair's invitation
to slump in a heap or sleep in a hump.

I'm by contrast on a hardbacked chair
sitting prim and tightarsed as Britannia
with a shield of books and a chewed biro.

The argument we're having is unravelling
the ends that look so odd now
they're asunder, we can only wonder

how they ever did get joined together.
It seems we've unwound an ampersand and
pulled it like a cracker. On the third chair

the black-and-white cat and the white-and-black,
love-locked in a tricky double-helix,
keep licking each other's necks.

CONFESSION

The stuffed armadillo in its glass case
was the one thing fashioned to withstand
the blue of Mr Glazier's gaze.

Matron found this beneath your mattress. And
don't please tell me you've never seen it.
(I hadn't—not *that* one anyway.) *How old*
are you?—Eleven, sir.—So young and yet
so . . . shall we call it erudite? He turned
his weight towards the centre-fold spread:
legs that parted on dark dishevelled gold
and something bared and complex as a bud
half-blocked by his tweed sleeve and fat hand.

My denials made no more headway than
the armadillo in its belljar;
those hard claws scampering on the unscratched floor
were after something unobtainable like air.

Out of the windows I saw
the tall prefects playing bowls
under the statues of Greek philosophers
girding their toga'd loins and waving scrolls.

FETISH

That my first car, at thirty, should be fifth-hand,
a filthy patchwork of worn azure and bare zinc
and amateur spray-jobs like a subway wall,

appeals to my pride as a failed consumer.
Its faults I can cherish as if they were my own.
What does it matter that its lights are dimmer,

that each year a psoriasis of rust is rising
from its mudguards and its bodywork has travelled
countless kilometres from the original plan

when something inside miraculously
keeps going, going against the predictions
of its detractors—who are vile, and legion.

What does it matter it's not long for this world
when shards of it, its polished tyres for instance,
are primed to outlast the most resistant

and cared-for of my bodily remains.
There is so much to thank it for. It makes
my superfluous entrances and exits

possible, that would have been difficult
or undreamt-of, otherwise. It gives me
the illusion of progress and takes away thought

like television, replacing it with a system of mirrors,
reflexes and recognitions like a Kertesz photo.
It takes me places that I thought I'd never see

even though seeing them is not that different
from not having seen them—but who's to say
if experience doesn't help, doing nothing does?

It teaches me a deep metallic pillow-talk
of mounting lugs drive shafts seal lips and bleeder valves
and, in the stale inches of the traffic jam,

lipreading, hand gestures and slow footwork.
It provides a haven to smoke and talk in
when there's rain, a host to our interminable

arguments, a roadside seat, a mobile cupboard,
a crystal kiosk and a rubbish dump,
civilization emptied of its discontents.

But what would happen if it left me?
I heard you say just now it's dangerous
and drives you mad to fall in love at thirty.

SIGNS

That May the neighbourhood showed signs
of a commercial revival: the newsagent
moved into blue videos and stocked his fridge
with sweating cartons of tropical fruit juice.
(Unshaken, my theory of separation held
a layer of mango lay above the guava.)
Then the derelict garage became a furniture salesroom
—in just two months a team of acrobats
who'd rigged clone buildings in a score of cities
had clad its angles in carob-coloured plastic.

Could these be the first tender shoots
of economic growth the government had promised,
a yuppie crop to sprout when people stopped
pricing themselves out of jobs? The nation
rising from the brine with its missile-launchers
still untarnished. Behind the stern blue drapes
of the Tory Conference you could feel
the pocked walls mouldering to the loud applause.
In June, I had the impression the world'd turned puce,
shiny as a burst bubo or a chancre.

I was still gingerly buffing the first sentence
of my novel, like that character in Camus:
'That May the neighbourhood showed signs
of an unprecedented decay . . .' In the Middle Ages
the local park had been a plague-pit.
Now gangs of stray dogs worried lone strollers.
Even the ladybirds started maneating
starved of aphids by the pesticides.
The asbestos partitions in our new co-op house
became my intimate terror. I stuffed my face

into a black gas-mask shaped like a pig's snout
to root them out but the white fibres settled,
and waited, on every upturned plane.
The old oak girders had taken such a clouting
from the lorries that I slept on a gradient
and woke at a slant. Only the clouds
through the tilting windows seemed
at the right angle, inflated, unperturbed.
Two bags of plaster hardened in the hallway
spilling, at contact, a weak cloud of dust.

Exposed brickwork above the kitchen sink
rained red on the plates and stayed unrepaired.
Something stank in the garden: a fat rainbow trout
our drunk co-tenant had forgotten to cook
and was too unsentimental to bury;
we found it among the hollyhocks, a new life
seething under its flushed silver scales.
I was subject to the flamingo tint
you chose for your fringe—it was so
alternative, it made the rest of you look orange.

Walking with you, I wondered if
all that reflected glory might prove dangerous.
But it didn't take you long to work out
that I was a grey element, unsupportive,
contentious, cold and crypto-chauvinist . . .
when you just about had me summed up
you left me for a classical guitarist.
I took up the tin-whistle in earnest
but then you left him for an American carpenter.
I worried about the mythic trees you used to paint.

Outside, some kids, browned off with the phone-booth,
had snapped a sapling rowan in half.
They may have thought they were putting it out
of its misery—a lifetime beautifying the lorry-route
to the A1: arboreal euthanasia.
Rowans were sacred to the Celts who planted them
one side of their thresholds; the punishment
for stripping bark off trees was to flay alive
the culprit and use his skin to bandage the pith.
Virulent Manx justice! I would have liked

to stick the tree together with glue,
to lift those orange berries from the dust.
In the main boulevard of Havana, they have armed
policemen to guard the last Cuban mahogany trees
so maybe, there, some Celtic strain survived.
The Local Residents' Group was sending round
its poison print-outs, hectoring against
the evils of stone-cladding, having seen
property prices drop. Their enthusiasm
for a Neighbourhood Crime Watch scheme

was a rage for Order: we were all to lurk
behind curtains, our eyes peeled like white tomatoes.
They rounded off with a scabby diatribe
against the black choir in the Seventh Day Adventist Church
whose voices lit the evenings. The rest of the summer
flounced by in a succession of street festivals,
marches and concerts while somewhere else
in the city power was steadily amassed
by those who didn't wear badges or link arms
and had squads to spare to send out against pickets.

CORNBRIDE

The cornfield
is a gold comb
or a sunned fleece
the wind grooms

to a shadow
or perhaps a cloud
the wind kites
is trailing shadow

miles behind
as a bride trails
broad muslin veils
in daylight outside

though already
she's being led
with a light tread
along the aisle.

EARTHBOUND

She lay mute as an Old Testament sacrifice;
nothing so abundant as a thicket—
but barbed wire, a secular parallel,
the sheep had snagged her horn on, days before

judging by the jaundiced eyes and tantrum
of panic, perfunctorily abandoned,
when we came by. She must have tried grazing
the wrong side, where the promised pastures grow,

and ended up like this—involved
in a fatally elegant metal-puzzle.
Like Samson, the secret of her strength
was her undoing. Plush Derry peat

that let its coppery fluid seep
round every footprint till the ling sprung back
had stained the once-white fleece with darkness
in a rising watermark. Keck-handed

Samaritans, we unwound the ravelled horn and stood
rooted as the sheep reared in reverse out,
Lazarus-like, from the bared earth's open trench
and, as if the wire's plucked note, running its length

faint as a pulse, had knelled for no one else,
her lungs rasped like broken bellows, her back legs
braced to uphold the body's earthbound weight
then let the burden fall back on its own.

CARGO

Two paunchy barrels
with distended staves
brewed the rainflow
from the greenhouse roof.
Cutlasses of thorn
stood guard at one.

Motionless I'd peer
into the other
at the quicksilver
tails vanishing
azure of beetles
and my eyes floating

half-closed, Chinese
on the green dome
of the waterdark
like two canoes
conveying jewels
to their own kingdom.

RITE DE PASSAGE

The foreign place-names sped past like blurred print—
solemn, unpronounceable inscriptions—
as she sat with the terracotta jar
between her knees and spelt out the sign
on the steel tag screwed to the window-frame:
NE JETEZ AUCUN OBJET PAR LA FENÊTRE.
Her knuckles whitened round the neck of the jar.
Some corner of a foreign field . . . he never
gave a toss for that. He'd sold his medals
for coppers under the sign of the three brass balls
and come out beaming—a weight off his chest—
but the first time back since the last war,
his first 'jaunt' abroad to stop like a clock
not to cough wake up wink not to nod or grin
not to anything anymore—that was more than bad luck;
it was everything weightless and insipid
like mothwings crushed in linen or love-letters burned
to a talcy wad. She expected something
more cumbersome to fetch back. At Dover,
where the gulls fought and the passengers filed
toward Customs, she didn't join the queue
and her granddaughter, guarding the suitcase,
watched her walk back slowly to the quay,
stand, unbalanced, peering from the edge
then pour him out like an offering to the birds.
He rested a while on the oil-film
faintly and a little aloof, a grey smudge
fading and darkening into the waters.

MERSEY PLUMAGE

There's a stretch of mud and redrock
over the railings down a ten-foot drop
the river gradually lays bare
when the sea breathes back its waters.
Between the worn down mounds of rock
the bricks and bottles and bladderwrack,
the stranded pools and puddles wear a skin
of marbled vivid oil. It's the water's
coat-of-Joseph and its Nessus-shirt
only the hardy survive: odd pink bivalves
mottled crabs, incorrigible lugworms.
Each winter I come back, hear underfoot
the crackle of glass and shell, the clutched
slurp of mud and the seaweed's wheezing vesicles
disgorging sewage. I follow again
the familiar profile of the skyline,
its comb of coolingtowers and chimneys
bathed in their vapours, brewing up
one more prismatic sunset. Everything
is covered with a loving grey drizzle
the gull's wings cut right through
en route for the Pier Head where they assemble
skirling the ferries into harbour
from Dublin, Belfast, the Isle of Man.
The gulls are as usual here as the stones
they could have hatched from, but this year
I'm sure there are more birds than ever:
knots peeping into the air in flocks
at the first crank of a dockside crane;
mallards at anchor in the khaki tide,
even a curlew nearby, heard not seen.
It's as if the despaired-of dove returned
with a sprig of olive in her bill
or the tamed familiar Liver Birds
had shaken their sooty pinions free
of slaveships, hovels and merchant banks,
the one-way-deal of industry.
No, it's hard to imagine the Mersey clear
divested of petrochemicals at last
a home and sanctuary for all,

with the first salmon for centuries
passing the estuary, heading inland
and all that broken glass blended and rounded
making a rainbow of the riverbed.

LANDING

I travelled in a bucket strapped below
a vast balloon like an eyeball
over the roofs of Paris, taking photographs

and over alleys narrow as the makeshift coffins
the Communards lay in with numbered tags
around their necks, till the wind blew me

clattering northwards past the gunboats
and the crowds on the quayside waving flags.
Then in a cold dark haywire cloud of rain

I saw the India Buildings and the Pier Head
and followed the river widening to Garston.
Between the listing buoys and sandbanks

two mulish tugs were pulling a tanker
loaded with glass from Pilkington's.
On the far shore, the sky at Port Sunlight

was singed by a petrol flame while the near
green railings on the riverbank
were matted black from the high tide's oil clods.

I saw a man bent by work so double
his face looked at his navel where he held
a mirror to show him the road ahead.

I could taste iron in the air, and naphthalene.
Either the rocks were bleeding or the horizon
was on fire. *This is the Stain of Empire*

said one sign with a skull above a knife and fork.
Another claimed in a script of faded gold:
Everything that has been will be restored.

A third one merely pointed to the playground
where the docks used to be . . . now couples raced
in coaltrucks round the wasteland railway.

Then I landed like a silk bomb by the glasshouse
and opened the chipped door onto daylight
smashing light off every kindled edge and curve

—lace-like ferns and forests with mansized leaves
grew round the aisles where everybody was
wild in the humming lattice of the dome.

II
LOST CITIES

A LOST CITY

Heaven is the country of the exiles.
They travelled here for refuge or for rest,
To learn the language or to taste the fruit.
Years pass. A cloud occludes the mountain's foot
And the road home is overgrown with mist,
The white edges of a virgin forest
Neither daytrip nor exodus defiles.

The bread is good and bitter but still leaves
The palate aching for an absent flavour.
The shopping malls have windows where you find
Instead of your own face, a heedful neighbour
Whose joy to find you may be just as feigned.
Is your face too, so transfigured and tanned?
Less old each day, less coarsened by beliefs?

Perhaps this isn't heaven after all.
The walls are veined with rose and polished beryl
—An ichor that you don't know how to tap.
New arrivals are treated with such awe,
Robed in colours, in light, as if each step
They take will help us trace some lost Before
Which if it ever was we can't recall.

ANOTHER LOST CITY

The frockcoated twins, with their boxer's shoulders,
Have parked their hearse outside the jewellers.
I steel myself to look them in the eyes.
Behind smoked glass, their three dark brides are swathed
In ivory satin. If only they'd escape!
The sea clops and blisters like boiling clay.
On the quayside the guards have laid a table
And lean to feed the new guests sharkmeat
From pitchforks. Others stroll along the seafront
On living stones the mottled colour of skin.
The sounds they make are not the same as words.
But you can't complain when the air they breathe
Is molten glass and the guidebook has
No sooner opened than burst into flame.

DECADENCE

It was the time of day when the soul speaks Latin
with a Gothic slur, and sees in every direction
an evening made of basil and magenta.

There was no breeze, and we were walking
by the canals and office-blocks of Carthage.
You were in a sour mood and foresaw

only war and burning, widows and orphans.
I suggested we stop at a bar for sherbert
—the latest thing, sprinkled with ginger.

From there, we could see the queen on her terrace
sporting her would-be wedding gown, its train
of damask roses twined with ears of corn.

The light took on a green tinge and a drunk
ex-mercenary kept muttering about drift-lines
where banded kraits would coil to clean their scales

—diamonds glittering in the sea-junk.
It made no sense to me, but sense
was not what I was after. I wanted dreams.

As dusk drew in its final flecks of gold
I felt the black north couching in my bones.

DOUBLE EXPOSURE

'Ah, the Life of Reilly!' you sighed between courses
—the jug of local white now down at heel,
the shells on the side-plate empty of all
but the finest ligament to show they were
once someone else's living-room.
Which made us burglars. I drank to Reilly
whoever he was, and followed his career
out of the dumps into some beachside bower
like here at Charybdis . . . cane chairs out on the piazza,
June midnights and the spangled pleasure-seekers
creasing the moonlit waters with silver arms
to the music of a chocolate advert. Did Reilly wait
for a red hand to crash down through the palmfronds
and pluck him from his halcyon pied-à-terre?

By the cashtill was a fishtank which a crayfish
had all to itself with eyes like black pods
fixed on the other side of the glass.
One large antenna snapped, two thin quiffed horns still
questioned the echoes in the ripples off the glass
made by its crooked legs that strummed across
its underbelly—such delicate pale treasure!
Stippled with terracotta markings,
could anything earthly ever be so exposed?

MARGIN

Some played volleyball using fishing nets;
some drank cans of *Perroni*; others searched
inland for flints and sources of clear water.

I wandered by the shore towards the harbour
and the blind lighthouse of Palinurus,
and found a dolphin turning at the tide's hem

bluntly, its skin fraying on the sharp stones;
then the stringy, knifed wheeze of the helmsman
came back from the shadows and a light struck

fire through the mute larynx of the rock
at Cumae—the mad woman humming just to calm him:
That cruel place will always bear your name.

NOSTALGIA

I woke drenched in sweat and homesick
for nowhere I could think of, a feeling
scuffed and quaint as farthings or furlongs.

Then I remembered the room of the sirocco
in a Sicilian palace made of pink volcanic sugar.
There was a scent of waxed oak and pistachios.

Two maids were making up our nuptial bed,
smoothing the white linen with their dark hands.
You'd never have finished finding fault in their work

if I hadn't intervened, so that you turned on me
saying *Their family were turnip doctors
at the time of the Bourbons*—an old enmity then,

and more imperious even than pleasure.
How to get out of that windowless room,
with not one of its walls adjoining the air

was all I could think of, from that point on.
Your voice pursued me down the marble stairway:
Don't think you'll ever find a home again!

MEMORY

The staff are picketing the pleasure gardens
of the Baia Hotel with placards.
The sun is trying to melt the rocks.

The Hohenzollerns and the Hohenstaufens
are having their annual conference inside
while their saffron-tinted, air-conditioned coaches

loaf in the parking lot above the cliff
and their drivers try to read the placards
—something about the bay being soiled,

a filter, and embezzled public funds.
I've got to know each curve of this coast road
as the car hairpins like a cardiograph.

(From a distance, it is gently bow-shaped.)
I know where a barn-owl nests and where
the agaves leap from their rootstock toeholds

and could tell of the netted lemon groves
that hesitate on parapets so narrow
you want to talk them back to safety;

and of the watchtowers underwater,
the window where a moray eel is curled . . .
but I won't—this need to depict

is just a weakening of the hold I have
on that rockface, a fatal stepping-backwards
onto glazed blue tiles that are tiles of air.

ENCLOSURE

Every part of the city was under the one roof:
lawcourts, infirmaries, boulevards, the squares. I kept
going up and down steps in search of a skylight.

Strollers walked their turtles on a lead
and the pace of life on the arcades was slow
to fit the stores where nothing was for sale

for everything had been bought a long time ago
and was closed in numbered cases, even the statues.
For everyone was a tourist in their own home

and because the streets had all become interiors
each room served as a thoroughfare.
I felt lost in the library of borrowed stones

and took you to the room up in the tower
where we found a window over a tiled roof
some derelicts were perched on, drinking wine.

NEWS FROM NOWHERE

Whoever it was put nowhere on the map
as a place to visit or plan to visit
or have a streetplan of, was losing heart.

He had considered every means of transport,
air-routes and sea-routes, and found them wanting.
And every road he chose led back to Rome,

a Rome not quite the same Rome as before,
where senators barked from curtained litters,
but still bleeding the provinces and setting fire

to anywhere that failed to pay its tribute
or didn't heap its trays with fruit and meat
or tried to cut loose from the coils of law.

And nowhere was that place just out of reach
of Caesar's wrath, where no one is bled dry
and bread is broken for each one to eat.

III

AXLE-TREE

I lurk like a stowaway in the dark threshold
of your block of flats and wait for a sign.

I park my wreck beside the lorries that slouch
at the curb till dawn, laden to the tusks
with mahogany logs from Senegal.

At the docks, just a caber's toss away,
where row after row of raw pink Fiats
are waiting for Legion to possess them,

they season in heaps and no sooner move
than they come to a halt, as if obeying
some natural imperative. Your balcony

gives on timber seeping resin
in the moonlight; the mountains bracketing
the bay's black waves as they fret

the sea-front and the frail hull
of the unfrequented *Nave-Ristorante*
moored under the Cement Factory's toxic plume.

It's all crammed-in like a tourist's map.
Nightshifts, headlamps and the desultory tide.
The palm fronds shrugging on the promenade.

Loosed from the shaggy leggings of those logs
I expect a windfall of treesnakes and insects
to seep through the holes of my peel-back roof.

Only last week a scorpion stung you.
Starting as a fire on the side of your thigh
it came to a head in a charred violet point . . .

you became irascible and superstitious
and dreamed of a horrible martyrdom.
You felt my star-sign made me somehow to blame

as if I'd hired a familiar for the crime.
My car fell under suspicion. You began to call it
The Touring Insect House, checking the seats

and shadows on entering, where before
you'd merely likened it to the bin-skips
with their beds of decomposing ash-blue mulch.

I've my doubts too. Do lovers use it by night?
Its suspension is not what it used to be.
Beer bottles, cigarette packets with odd

brand-names, chewed gum-wads: all add up to something
—nocturnal depredations! Anything could live there
biodegrading, unobserved, while the rear-mirror

makes headlights flare like stars snapped out of fixity
and the hewn trunks seem lengths of a broken axle
around which once the leaf-green planet turned.

DE-SIGNIFIERS

Rust and dry-rot and the small-jawed moth
are our best friends and they wish us well,
undoing the fabric of our heaven.

They correspond to something inside us
that doesn't love the works our hands have made
—wire-cutters, pick-locks, saboteurs.

'Are you building a good memory to have of me?'
you once asked as though I'd just begun
a papier-maché Taj Mahal.

I keep a cardboard box of newspapers
in the cupboard so everything that's happened
is safe from pulp mills and the record-shredders

but all the while in the dark the silverfish
and woodlice are at work on the word,
its dot matrix. Living on what seems to us

dust, they profit directly from our negligence
and attention in general only provokes
their swerving, averting or curling-up manoeuvres.

Meaning? They roll it away and break it down
into unrecombinable fragments
like fatigue in our metal or cancer in concrete.

TIME PIECE

Redefining the concept of time
hourglass, sundial and clockface give way
to this queue of agitated digits
above the buttons on the rented tv.
Neat and absolute, a usurping lineage
the hours that aren't don't wait like courtiers
their turn to be—it's more of a countdown
in reverse, an accumulation of useless numbers . . .

The only wristwatch I ever had was passed
down to me, along with a stamp collection,
by a great-uncle, the way that objects
the dead are disencumbered of are left
to haunt the living. Both bound in leather
they were manly items meant to guide
me through a life of anxious gathering.
(My sisters didn't figure in the will.)

The stamps got intercepted but the watch
plagued me like a treacherous intimate
with its pipsqueak commentary—its only fuel
the money-sign between finger and thumb.
Too fiercely wound, the little chariot's springs
collapsed but each time came back good as new
until that hour we parted company.
It was the Twilight of the Hippies.

My negligence abetted the theft of time.
I almost connived to be free at last
of its guilt-ridden discourse and hand-cuff clasp.
Give or take five minutes it was ten o'clock
but it could have been any hour of the day
when the watch was lifted from the dormitory
upstairs—an unsegregated sea of mattresses
at the Amsterdam *Sleep In* whilst I was eating

a yoghurt muesli from a plastic carton
in the dim stadium of the underground canteen
where the bongs and chillums puffed like thuribles
and the hash haze held time in a trance.
Since then the problem has been how to
reconcile the two realms: the shrill machine
that rules us and that timeless zone the days
with glittering axles wheel through without tracks.

NOTHING REALLY

My fob-watch stopped at that betrayal:
the two of you clinging together
like straws on the sofa. I found
the secondhand snagged on the hourhand
so I opened the glass front
and gently bent the hourhand
to arch its passage round the day.
When I turned the knurled knob, the minutehand
swept round the dial and the hours
ran after but the winding mechanism
was blocked, time hadn't budged an inch;
so I prized open the backlid
with my fingernail and saw
the whole jewelled affair, a little
Cartesian universe, absolutely paralysed.
It was luck, I suppose,
that with the slightest
touch of a matchstick on the mainspring
it began to pulse again, ticking away
as if nothing had happened.

ODRODEK II

It is hard to describe me. And why should I try?
When the cleaners have gone home

I trek through the rubber-tread corridors
rolling on my faces like a marble ashtray.

I sprout cilia or a pseudopodium,
fed on burn-bags and administrative boredom.

Everything stale, glazed, exhaled, used-up, left-
over sustains me. I grow star-shaped and lucid

like a cog at the core of the system.
Suavely, I propagate in the tepid

pipes and filters of the air-conditioning.
I breathe the greasy dust of the lift-shaft

dating its bouquet with my carbon palate
and feel the shadow of the ironweight

plumb through the floors on its frayed cable
as the bare bulb rises like a yellowed eye.

Moiling in the dark of utility
I am attuned to the subtle traffic of the air.

You will not be rid of me. I've become
computer-adept and user-friendly.

My image flickers and your days are numbered.

A CZECH EDUCATION (1948–)

for Lucie

'All that remains of Clementis is the cap
on Gottwald's head.'—Milan Kundera

A frontispiece for one of the standard school texts
showed Gottwald donning a Russian cap Clementis,
the Jewish partisan, has handed him
in a sweeping gesture—reminiscent of Raleigh
or Garibaldi before Victor Emmanuel—
a history teacher's favourite anecdote.

When Clementis had been hung for treason
at the front of the new edition was Gottwald
in the same photograph and hat, but his righthand man
has done the bunk. Call it ingratitude
or history's trick photography
the hat he wore no longer had a story.

When not long after Stalin's funeral
Herr Gottwald died still dogging his master's heels
they built a gimcrack shrine up Zizkov Hill
near the heart of old Prague
to house his glorious memory and corpse.
In life a puppet, in death a waxwork doll.

He was embalmed after the fashion of Lenin, or almost;
only the State's unpractised taxidermists
lacked the Kremlin's expertise with death.
Either that, or there was a Joker in the pack.
As Gottwald began to rot, less and less
of the man seemed to be on display.

More and more people heard and a series
of regrettable jokes corrupted the young.
Filing past the much-revered carcass
these jokes, like luxuries smuggled across
a guarded border, simultaneously overwhelmed
two girls on a school outing in '58.

The pious hush in there had been too much for them.
Frogmarched out, shaking all too audibly
they were disciplined next day for their calculated
insult to the People, their act of vandalism.
Gottwald then fell out of favour.
After '68 his punctured image was reinflated

to its former eminence in all the history books.
(That bubbling noise again: *'Bobok! Bobok!'*)
His poor bruised rancid body wheeled
up and down and in and out of state
as if damned to perpetual motion—decay
always advancing on cosmetics.

And those beleaguered trimming textbook hacks
dodging, veering and double-backing
to readjust the nation's history syllabus
can best be seen as hapless coffin-bearers
stumbling up a downward escalator
as one more blemished limb breaks out of cover.

IN FRONT OF THEM

Those who are about to die sit for their photograph
in newly-issued boots, their brows puckered and bleached
against the sun. Some smoke pipes but all of them are smiling

—either smiling or tensing the muscles around their mouths
as a prelude to smiling, not knowing the shutter had fallen.

IL CAPITANO

He keeps a dark shed by the beachhuts and boathouses
smelling of diesel and damp wool;
there's a yellowed notice tacked to the door
in a strange hand, or a strange tongue like the babble
of waves on pebbles, cursives of broken shell.

Bound in his nets and tackle, he carries a trident
to tap the ground in the tireless pacing
that keeps him always in sight of the sea
where the spiny rocks sift back the waves
like krill-less drizzle from the teeth of whales.

The villagers tell how once, years back,
he commanded a vessel wrecked miles out
and drifted days on a fragment of deck.
Ever since his rescue he's lived like the last man alive
in this coast resort buzzing with tourists and Vespas.

He was washed up here like the rest of us
by seed, tide, trade or fate but clearly lives,
oblivious of custom, under a different sky
—the stars urgent and legible; the miles of black salt
crashing into coves, his intimate blueprint.

It's said that sometimes he sights a ship
far out in the blue and foams with an exquisite
panic of recognition. Dropping his stick
he thrashes through the waves like a fierce child
till the fishermen gently drag him back again.

SIGN LANGUAGE

The deaf-mute fisherman sits in his beached boat
with the net he's mending looped round both big toes
and his lefthand thumb while his right hand weaves
in and out. Air and water crash in soundless waves
through the spaces where his livelihood will catch,
the fishes whose new names I'm slowly learning:
merluzzo, alice, dentice, pesce spada . . .
Seeing me reading, he signs that books are better
—what he earns in a day I spend in an hour
eating fish at the restaurant he supplies.

Motorini swarm in from the cities
of the plain, from the little badlands
under the shadow of Vesuvius. Then when the bars
are closed, the cars in the car park rock like boats,
their windows taped with *Lo Sport* or *L'Unità*
and I see him picking his way home
through the refuse of a beach-culture
with nothing but a bemused welcoming smile
—though when he stops outside his door I'd swear
he's talking to himself with his fluent hands.

DARKNESS IN THE MEZZOGIORNO

Rubbish clots the courtyard's fountain sculpture
of Neptune clouting a triton with a fishbone.
There's a smell of rotting cuttlefish
off the cobbles, and an iridescent sludge
of rosy scales and silver fishes' eyes. The sea
is everywhere, and nowhere visible, like God.
It sweats through the walls where sand from the sea
was used four centuries ago for stucco.
These alleys where the local kings and *pezzi grossi*
hung out from the verdant balconies
are still rich as any royal family
in the underwater categories of crime,
and seethe with bullet-headed shoals
of *ruffiani, spacciatori, camorristi.*
In winter the prostitutes sit warming
their slack calves over a fire of fruit crates.
A lack of expectation lights
along the false blonde's unbruised olive eyes.
Everything that happens happens on the streets
or overlooking them. There's no elbow-room
under the sign AREA DI MANOVRA:
for the old men playing *scoppa* where
the pavement ought to be; for cars
that back up the way they came or
airwaves jammed with radios and rows;
no room to retreat where history
has made a fig-sign at the private life.
Lost empires jostle in the cellarage
and layer after layer of colonists lie shelved
under the cobbles with their dialects
and utensils—Roman, Saracen and Spaniard—
their rubbish and their triumphs petrified:
jewel-hilted daggers and medical tracts
rhymed in Latin; lacquered fans and vessels carved
for Christendom by Arab ebonists . . .
down there are knots that no one can undo
wounds fingerprints and pomegranate seeds,
bedheads and olivestones and shoulderblades
in sheets of salt hid from the light of day.

MERMAID

My mistake was not to leave a breathing space,
a vacuole for firing in the kiln
but I was only thinking of the shape
she'd grow into, sleek and seal-grey, her flanks
basted with a patina of sea-slime.
She did not look like something that could last,
washed-up, drying from the outside inwards,
a shade more pallid every day, but the limbs
I was lucky with—the arch of the back,
the balance of her small provocative head
and the breasts on which I'd lavished
more than a cameo-maker's care. The tail
was cleftless, with the usual scales
etched by a pin. So how did mermaids mate?
No doubt they found some way, agonizingly
metamorphic, for their cast-ashore princes
though I strayed no nearer a solution
than the faintest hint. On that coastal windowsill
she sat battening on the muzzled crash the waves
made on the rocks, draining in tiny rills.

When she broke she broke across the navel
in a break so fine she could still balance
without glue on those stunning ichthyian hips.
The second crack came in an argument
at the curve where her knees would have been.
There was a storm and the sea crashed against the mole.
Then, when we moved to make way for the rich
summer tenants, among boxes of stones and shells,
the beachcombed chips off seaworn tiles,
she took more punishment—her nose crumbled
and her face became the fate of Cresseid
in the drypoint version of Henryson.
She stayed among discarded things
stacked in the back of my battered Citroen,
its scalloped bonnet like the boat of Venus,

until the day the seastorm peeled the roofs
from the beachhuts and a great wave palled
the piazza with saltwater, waistdeep
where the cars were parked . . . there, in the boot,
I found a layer of sand and nothing more
than a grey trace, a silt of potter's clay.

OXFORD POETS

Fleur Adcock
James Berry
Edward Kamau Brathwaite
Joseph Brodsky
Basil Bunting
W. H. Davies
Michael Donaghy
Keith Douglas
D. J. Enright
Roy Fisher
David Gascoyne
Ivor Gurney
David Harsent
Anthony Hecht
Zbigniew Herbert
Thomas Kinsella
Brad Leithauser
Derek Mahon

Medbh McGuckian
Jamie McKendrick
James Merrill
Peter Porter
Craig Raine
Christopher Reid
Stephen Romer
Carole Satyamurti
Peter Scupham
Penelope Shuttle
Louis Simpson
Anne Stevenson
George Szirtes
Grete Tartler
Edward Thomas
Charles Tomlinson
Chris Wallace-Crabbe
Hugo Williams